I0517389

A Season in Lowertown

A Season in Lowertown

David Blaikie

Wet Ink Books

First Edition

Winner of the 2021 Don Gutteridge Poetry Award

 Wet Ink Books
www.WetInkBooks.com
WetInkBooks@gmail.com

Copyright © 2022 Wet Ink Books
Copyright © 2022 David Blaikie

All rights revert to the author. All rights for book, layout and design remain with Wet Ink Books. No part of this book may be reproduced except by a reviewer who may quote brief passages in a review. The use of any part of this publication reproduced, transmitted in any form or by any means, electronic, mechanical, photocopied, recorded or otherwise stored in a retrieval system without prior permission in writing from the publisher or a licence from The Canadian Copyright Licensing Agency (Access Copyright) is prohibited. For an Access Copyright licence, visit: www.accesscopyright.ca or call toll free: 1.800-893-5777.

A Season in Lowertown
by David Blaikie

Cover Image – Susan Rosidi
Cover Design – Richard M. Grove
Layout and Design – Richard M. Grove

Typeset in Garamond
Printed and bound in Canada
Distributed in USA by Ingram,
        – to set up an account – 1-800-937-0152

Library and Archives Canada Cataloguing in Publication

Title: A season in Lowertown / David Blaikie.
Names: Blaikie, David, 1946- author.
Description: Poems.
Identifiers: Canadiana 20220217297 | ISBN 9781989786673 (softcover)
Classification: LCC PS8603.L297 S43 2022 | DDC C811/.6—dc23

In memory of Alden Nowlan (1933-1983)
who won the Governor General's Award for Poetry
and continues to inspire
new generations of poets and writers.

Table of Contents

Spirits

Shadowland

Moments

Farewell

Introduction

"To every thing there is a season . . ."

My season was in Lowertown in the 1970s, one of the oldest districts of Ottawa, just east of Parliament Hill and the Chateau Laurier Hotel, where the Rideau Canal tumbles through ancient locks to the Ottawa River – the neighbourhood where French and Irish immigrants drank and fought, and made the capital of Canada to rise from the northern wilderness.

"A time to be born . . ."

I was new to Ottawa, having moved to Ontario from the Maritimes only a couple of years before, and was just out of a marriage I'd gotten into too young. I wanted nothing more than to lose myself and Lowertown was perfect, unpretty and undomestic, before the developers arrived and created the Byward Market of today. In those days, Lowertown still had the feel of early Canada, its founders and its scoundrels, loggers who danced and drowned on log booms, nuns and prime ministers who tramped its streets, and the ghost of Colonel John By, the sadistic genius who built the entire canal system in six short years – at the cost of a thousand dead labourers.

"A time to break down . . ."

Across the river from Lowertown lay *the Quebec side* and the city of Hull (known today as Gatineau), an enclave of wild night life, thanks to liquor laws that let bars stay open until three a.m., two hours later than *the Ontario side*. And a little further east sprawled the working-class neighbourhood of Vanier, formerly Eastview, which also teemed with night life. I embraced it all, the grit and grime, the French and Victorian architecture, the bars, the taverns, the all-night diners and hotels with creaking beds.

"A time to cast away stones, And a time to gather stones . . ."

I wept in Lowertown, I danced there. It exists within me still. These poems recount that season.

David Blaikie

Flight

Trumpets

I worked odd hours then
and drank a lot
the bottomless
drinking of being young
and running from a place
I should not have gone
that day with her
on a riverbank
in wafting country air
swearing it would be for life
when I felt I'd hardly been born
rebellion hissing like a fuse inside
the times blowing trumpets in my ears
Kerouac still alive then
men about to fly to the moon
and put big footprints there
I'm not sure I was thinking
at all, the minister in his collar
so black and white
with his *Book of Common Prayer*
I still hear his voice
intoning those ancient words
if any man can show just cause
... let him speak now or else
... or else .... *I do, I do*
doubt swirled like dust inside

Blue

I see it yet, that *Dodge Dart* day
of powder blue and streamers
elm trees nodding at an eggshell sky
the river sliding away
her eyes alight
the wind soft in her hair
and that white dress
which sighed so on her body
me, I had a chain
about my neck
that I'd put on by myself
as I stood there
in that quivering air
of cars on summer grass
family, friends, and god
gathered round
and heard her recite each word
as if carving it in stone
I told myself I'd settle in
and we walked from there into life

Ring Dance

she was all a man could ask
a spirit unafraid and clear
I'd look at her
looking out at the harbour
in the city where we started out
waters choppy and gray below
and I'd wonder
what was wrong with me
a thing that circled
like gulls inside
I'd see those ships turn out
and away, and be ambushed
by the line of a song
we'd drink, and go to bed
pour sex into the silence
then rise and work another day
I wore that yellow ring
a while, but it burned
like a coal on my hand
we unravelled, sure and slow

Gone

five years later I was in a room
and she was on the coast
tall trees tilting
at an island sky
the Pacific at her toes
a jet plane gone
from the past and me
the brokenness and blur
I imagined her on a beach
somewhere
trying to untangle it all
time lapping in from Japan
a cove curling off
in waves of light
and threads of undertow
she bought herself a car there
and listened to Dory Previn
Mythical Kings and Iguanas
and pondered that poets
could hurt her more
than men who were rough
and fucked on the floor

Rum

I took a room on Friel Street
before it was Beausoleil
a worn-out place that felt
about right, furnished
to the specs of a classified ad
which wasn't much in those days
I found it on the morning
of the night I left the last time
the elevator empty
going down
the parking lot stilled below
headlights switching at three a.m.
through the black dark damp
of going
I slept in the car
with a bottle of rum
somewhere in the Gatineau Hills
pines and sumacs
wrapped around me
no memory of stars in the sky
the engine off, the windows cold
I wanted no one
and nothing to find me

Morrow

daylight hit the windshield pale
a spider staring in at me
as if sent by god and her
I saw guilt walk
with a thousand legs
down a sunlit wiper blade
dead bottle cobwebs in my head
that car a cocoon and jail
I knew exactly where she'd be
staring out a window
seven floors up
across an iron balcony
the Queensway waking
like a snake in the sun
exhaust boiling up and away
that rumbled sound
of too many wheels
whirling in the gut of day
and two yellow lines
like pick-up sticks
staring back empty
by a garbage bin
from the parking lot below

Verity

freedom doesn't tiptoe in
one easy bottle at a time
or fall in notes of tidy sequence
on the ear; it's a pitiless thing
when jarred this way
a riptide rising
in the folds of night
crashing on the beach at dawn
naked, defiant, full of glass
a billion bits of memory
flipping in the cold white foam
and the booming voice of now
calling in its wake
this is what you wanted
count it all

Night

Lowertown

the clock wrote shadows
on the walls of Lowertown
pushing the daylight back
in those scrawled out
chalkboard days
which was exactly
what I wanted
hardly thinking, hardly sleeping
waiting for night to fall
and set nerves alight
with pangs
of who knows what
just pull down the shades
unbake the glare of noontime sun
and flick the darkness on
inject both eyes with neon
and make briefcase interlopers
disappear with their shiny shoes
and business mouths
and every suit
that ever got worn in the name
of politics, god and commerce

Retreat

I hungered for the grit there
the plainness of the walls
the iron stairs, the shopworn halls
society was too prim
where I had been
the clutch of plants and linen
pillows perfect on a bed
knickknack things on shelves
and photos of the dead
the weight of spousal nouns
my husband and my wife
endearments
that billowed up
like debts upon my ear
too much, too soon
I needed ugly taverns for a while
bottles overflowing
clocks that let the nights
run free as stallions unto dawn
and mornings full of waking
to folly of my making
until that wind had blown

Ink

I ate at the old *New Moon* most days
or *Mellos,* a few doors up
wan old eateries
on Dalhousie Street where
I learned to say dal-*hoos*-zee
beans and eggs
in the small dark hours
when I returned from the bars in Hull
places good to sit a while
with women out to make a buck
and men with wallets on a chain
dark ink running
up and down their arms
before tattoos were common
anchors, aces, the *Jack of Hearts*
pin-up girls in sailor hats
scorpions, snakes, and *Mother*
in genuflecting font
I'd sit in a corner, or off at the side
and take it all in
coffee, toast, tobacco smoke
the rustle of working clothes
cops now and then
who knew their place
as long as you knew yours
stray words adrift in fryer fat air
I was glad to be anonymous there
sense the code inside
the small talk, as I made my way
one night at a time
to a place I could not see
and was in no rush at all to find

Neon

poetry fell from the streetlights
spinning in the spokes
of motorcycle wheels
dancing on the hood of cars
glinting from the cuffs
of big police as they strode
down streets and alleys
women prancing
like top ten songs
the lightning flare of sex
in their eye, tanned legs
striding across the screen of night
hair spilling down like foam
muscle cars and pick-up trucks
the *Raceway Tavern*
and the *Lafayette* - since 1849
salt in the beer joints
gritty as hell
and the peeler bar on York Street
dealers, vagrants, drifters
in a thousand shifting masks
and each official language
I wolfed it down like angel food

The Quebec Side

Ontario had a lot of the Queen then
and Quebec still some of the Pope
I cared little for either at the time
except for the difference
in last call at the bar
which was two hours later
on the Quebec side
and made me feel partial
to Catholics, the way
they could let it out all week
and confess to a priest on Sunday
the world writ deep
in their DNA
Marie pouring drinks
at the *Hotel Duvernay*
where we slipped off late
one night at closing
to a room somewhere
with a candle
and ate the dawn for breakfast
though Good Friday
came as a shock
the whole damn province
nearly half of Canada
coming to a halt at midnight
if just for one long barless day

Alan

I got to know a fellow in those days
passing through a time like me
a woman back there
in his rearview life
and photos of the kids he'd lost
a radio man
from out of the west
he could have been from a life
gone by, a drifter who
might have heard Guthrie sing
or set off in search of Rimbaud
his heart afire
with the whole shebang
yet the switchblade flash
of regret in his eye
for those babies so far away
he'd pull out the pictures
and gaze at them
in the barlight hours
of the places we knew
along Promenade du Portage
the strand that called
across the bridge each night
when Ontario went dark at one a.m.
and Anglo bars closed like clams

Slow dance

the *Standish Hall* and *Chez Henri*
the *Green Room* at *The Chaudière*
fists like fuses coiled there
and the *British Hotel* in Aylmer
a haunt of Sir John A. Macdonald
the *St. Louis* too
up dark Montcalm
where the bomber slept
before he blew himself up
on Parliament Hill
we knew all the Quebec side stops
places to flirt with danger
and buy our way out
with a round or two
or troll for women as loose as we
find a room and a bed for an hour
or a lady like Aline
a few years older
who smoked long cigarettes
and had radar eyes
I could feel across the room
she picked me out of the slow dance
dark; how could I ever forget?
took me back across the river
with her, and made cold nights
ring in Hintonburg
in that place she heated
with an oven and herself
above a funeral home on Fairmont
I can't send you home that way
she said, and she
was as good as her word

Want Ads

before the internet
sprang vice from jail
and killed the skin mags off
newspapers dressed themselves
in sanctimony
and swam in euphemism
fuddle duddle, rhymes with itch
yet covered the Irish Sweepstakes
15 to 2 shot wins
and pageants everywhere
Miss Canada, Miss Universe
the Renfrew dairy princess
and kept a corner
for small cramped ads
where code was king
nude hostesses, Bank at Walkley
Jenny's reduction special, to 2 a.m.
The Rub Club, 490 Rideau
lonely hearts and hustlers
WASP, conservative
searching for the right girl
black male model available
widow, attractive, forties
seeks tall gentleman
adult books, straight, gay
bizarre, 256 Albert Street
go-go dancers, full-time work
prime minister's
former limousine for rent
couples wanting to meet couples
marriage counselling
divorce assistance
hypnotist: smoking,
stammering, bedwetting
dial-a-bottle
the papers' most-read page
every day but Sunday

La Petite Auberge

for a while I went most nights
to *La Petite Auberge*
behind the *Hotel Duvernay*
a place where regulars liked to go
and bartenders lingered off shift
it had a small red light
up over the door
that hardly glowed at all
even in winter
when snow tumbled thick
through streetlights
and lay white along the alley
I got busted one night
by the drug squad there
they came flying in like hoodlums
slammed me against the wall
and rifled my pockets
for contraband, just itching
to show who was in charge
I was still sober
and had nothing on me
but I swore at a constable
named Menard
and he didn't take to that

Jail

next thing I knew
I was flat on the asphalt
beneath open patrol van doors
arms twisted back like pretzels
that big cop hissing down at me
Bastards? he said
in English so I'd understand
We gonna show you
and they took me off
to the dark Hull jail
somewhere up Saint-François
where woods circled in
like an accomplice
it could have been anywhere
I was shown to a place
with clanking doors
and matching metal decor
where eventually
they took the handcuffs off
and removed my belt
in the fluorescent glare
lest I hang myself
for swearing, I guess
and I spent a sleepless night
there, plotting naive revenge

Trial

I hired a lawyer who had
an office out Taché Boulevard
where West Quebec cars
sped by, and something
didn't feel quite right
he sat at his desk
regarding me
and took down a note or two
his briefcase clanked
he had ashes in his moustache
and insisted on his fees up front
then pleaded me innocent
to an obstruction charge
as if an Anglo could win in Hull
Menard on the stand as big as life
testifying under oath
that what I'd said in English
meant *fucking bastards* in French
and the judge didn't flinch at all
just found me guilty
with a little smile
and gave me a legal discharge
since I was a first offender
and had a job across the river

Spirits

Mirage

the thing about alcohol
is the way it can swirl in a glass
fling threads of light
across newfound lands
make a woman seem near
or far, or step with ease
into hanging stars
where *Bacardi* velvet reigns
turntables spinning
in the teeth of night
vinyl ablaze at two a.m.
like the holy rings of Saturn
even strong men
can be fooled by that
crushed like stone at morning
for there has never been
a reliable way
in the annals of all things alcohol
to splash in the brilliance
that reigns out there
and bring that treasure home

Jack

Kerouac danced on our tongues
back then, he had passed
not long before
we read everything he wrote
from Lowell to Big Sur
the continent unfolding
as if he knew each aching chord
Greyhound buses
crisscrossing the plains
of his Catholic-Buddhist soul
fingers ablaze with wine
and speed, typing his life
onto a teletype roll
On the Road was almost holy
Al sitting cross-legged
in his Centretown flat
three floors up a fire escape
that he'd sometimes climb
drunk in the dark
afire himself with red *Czechsardi*
a carton of *Belmonts*
askew on the carpet
I see him yet
one arm around the kitten
that he had for a time
the other waving a paperback
as he read aloud words
of hitchhike days
and light pole nights
on dusty roads
somewhere in California

purple dusk over tangerine
groves and long melon fields
... pressed grapes slashed
with burgundy ... the color
of love, and Spanish mysteries

Tangled

I wore *Blood on the Tracks* out
twice that winter
inside that Friel Street room
playing *Idiot Wind*
through long barbed hours
that hooked things
up from my gut
and spread them out
like scrap from a trunk
or things tossed off by a child
Buckets of Rain
sloshing through my brain
If You See Her Say Hello
that album in which
Dylan scraped his soul
a howl that came down
from the Iron Range
after he and his wife broke up
dawn poking in through
my window shade
like an intruder from Pestalozzi
that tower they called
a college back then
where kids got swallowed
in the sputum night
of needle point and dealers
I loved and hated every hour
I spent there, trying to
write my way to a better place
and a different point of view
Tangled Up in Blue

Saigon

days bristled with war and death
in that unsettled time
the awful camera that was Vietnam
images the eye cannot unsee
Quang Duc, the Buddhist monk
glistening in gasoline
engulfed in flame
on a street corner in Saigon
a suicide that shocked the world
and after that Kim Phuc
the napalm girl, just nine
arms flung out, her skin afire
fleeing naked down a road
and the pistol execution
of Van Lem, point blank
his face a thousand screams
unscreamed
as the bullet, flying yet
coursed through his brain
and we ate breakfast
half a world away
condemned America
smoked weed
watched Cronkite
speak the news each night
and heard Johnny Cash lament
a hundred fine young men
each week
as we fucked our way
through bewildered days
until Saigon finally fell
and it was over

Motorcycle

I had a motorcycle
that was good for the time
a bright chrome *Honda*
that I parked at the back
by a shivering poplar tree
where leaves fell off at autumn
and lay wet across
the gas tank and my mood
shade from buildings
pressing down
with wistful fishhook nerves
days already chill by mid-October
winds chafing in from Hudson Bay
you could sense the snow
that early, the unwished end
of the few short months
that northern riders know
flying with the big rigs
on the 401, white lines
snapping like popcorn
just daring the OPP
or turning off
into soft green hills
and climbing slow and lazy
through licorice turns of asphalt
past lakes as blue as jazz
up, up to the skies that monks
must crave, where evergreens
open in the Canadian Shield
and sunlight pours its hush
on Champlain Lookout

Bells

church bells pealed on Sunday
morning, it might have been
from *St. Brigid's*, ringing through
the streets of Lowertown
on the wreckage
of the night before, pale light
poking through pickled egg vomit
at the door of padlocked bars
condom foil and bottle caps
shards of busted glass
I'd think of those priests
in their long white robes
swinging that holy smoke
contraption, as if it
were some kind of cure
swallowing that useless little sip
of wine, and that nothing
wafer of bread, as I tossed
hung over in a sleeping bag
and pondered what it would take
to rise from the rumple
of that ill-lit room
and make my way
through the jigsaw day
to *Mellos*
for coffee in a ceramic mug
with toast and scrambled eggs

Before

Lowertown was nothing much
then, the raw old dump
it had always been, French
and Irish blood in its bones
whole blocks still caked
with grime and dust
from when Canada was born
it was just before
the developers came with
their aftershave and blueprints
politicians nodding at their heels
and remade it in the image
of the board of trade
sushi bars with flaunted ferns
big prices writ small
on dainty menus
at eateries with tablecloths
where trouble rarely happened
tourists wandering over
from the old stone pile
of Parliament Hill
to pay through the nose
for beaver tails, a pastry
some merchant dreamed up
or sangria with cheese
at chowder houses
where robot waiters
sang *Happy Birthday* and
served iffy fresh fish from P.E.I.
nine hundred miles away

Clarence Street

the *Chez Lucien Hotel* was near
its end, but had not yet been razed
sprawling in the tarnish
of Clarence Street
more stories than god could tell
I'd go there on long afternoons
entering by the corner door
and sit in the gloom with a beer
rough-toothed waiters
with x-ray eyes
they could see through walls
smell a dollar before it
stepped inside – the way
they protected the hookers there
alone at small dark tables
all smoke and painted nails
no one hardly saying a word
a juke box off at the side
glinting low, with songs
that felt dated even for the time
Elvis over and over again
the metronome beat
of *Suspicious Minds*
Sinatra crooning *High Hopes*
and Patsy Cline, *I Fall to Pieces*
in that voice that stopped
everything cold
coins clinking down
in a muted way
the street door opening
every now and then
and daylight gushing in
as everyone turned in unison to look
there was never any panic
they knew all the cops by name

Friel Street

crime churned into headlines
from my part of town
ten arrested in drug raids
just a couple of doors down
hashish, weed and LSD
plus some PCP that
was found in the stairs
while a man with a gun
a bit farther on
killed a girl from Britannia
and put her mother
in the Civic
with wounds to the head
car theft, coat thieves
lock pickers too
shoplifting a perfume
that hung in the air
two punks with a purse
tracked right to my building
after a woman at Christmas
was attacked near *The Bay*
and at a dark brick place
of unbroken gloom
near a corner store
where I often stopped
an arrest for a heist
at Ottawa Beef
where four hundred head
were slaughtered each day
and most jarring of all
a young man, twenty-two
pulled from a rooming house
when neighbours heard noises
and police found a ewe

Passage

Le Hibou still sat on Sussex then
night owls sketched above the door
awning rippling in the wind
not long before it closed
and took with it the aura
that great ones leave behind
Cohen in his early years
a bird on a wire himself
Judy Collins, who sang his lyrics
and pushed him to perform
Irving Layton, hair afire
searching for the messiah
so many scattered their light there
Joni Mitchell, skating away
Lightfoot bright with darkness
Neil Young, Bruce Cockburn
Sneezy Waters, Muddy too
and William Hawkins
there when it all began, the man
who stapled poetry to light poles
and drove a *Blue Line* cab
it's a place that I see yet
and a night still seared inside
Fraser & DeBolt on that small stage
so close I could have touched them
singing as if the current
of a thousand wires was coursing
through their veins

... lightning
brightly flashing ... thunder
shaking the floor ...
 ... I need your company ...
this storm shall surely pass

Apparitions

old streets remember corpses
for the longest time
ethers of disturbance
lingering at evening
in the eaves of tired houses
shapes that shift
where light leaves off
and strangled words begin
I felt it in the back streets
walking home, the rage
of Irish men who crossed the sea
and were abused by Colonel By
digging his damned canal
in this hard unbroken land
its heat in summer
sagging the strongest backs
mosquitos and malaria
winters hurled
unbearably from the sky
fists in ill-lit taverns
flying at French heads
and returned with equal force
maudit! câlice!
fabric ripping, teeth askew
the blackout dawn of morning
in this pitiless colony
so far from native shores
ghosts are born this way
and can live the longest time

Noel

I spent one Christmas Eve
across the river, where the only
revellers left were men
and a few stray women
whose lives were pared to that
the balm of familiar walls
and the warmth of alcohol
O Holy Night, this place
of little lights along the side
a Santa face bright red
reindeer in small hats
bottles in their lovely rows
low-lit, glinting, good
smoke from ashtrays rising
a sense of charity in the air
the mood more muted
than on normal nights
scraps of small talk
lapping in waves
along the darkened bar
this one from Trois-Rivières
that one from New Brunswick
another Tweed or Kingston
or some Ottawa Valley town
Blue Christmas playing softly
in the background
or *Silver Bells,* like ice
no one played *Silent Night*

Interlude

Al took up with Zou Zou
a singer with teenage sons
who lived in Westboro
estranged from a husband
who had a place downtown
and a mistress
younger and well-dressed
who drank with him
good liquor at his club
where he was a member
in good standing
known in his profession
I'd drive out there
on hot afternoons
when summer scorched the air
heat quivering the asphalt
on Richmond Road
and find them by the pool
with books and cigarettes
or when her sons were absent
hear an orchestra of mating
from an open upstairs window
it didn't last that long
but it was real, their way
with words, how she
touched him with a glance
and sang for him, her laughter
full and clear, a woman who
withstood the scorn of peers
to dally with a younger man
and reach for life again

Cold

winter squeezed the city
and its soul, white winds
piercing down
from hills across river
snow in swaths
that swallowed cars
and twisted through tall buildings
fraying flags on shivering poles
I'd sit inside that room
and hear pipes crack
or watch light play
through window frost
and wonder how the voyageurs
stared this merciless continent
down, the wilderness
of Canada long ago
its breath, its ice
that hour of cold
when the sun pulled back
its hand, and darkness
fell upon their loneliness
so that they could scarcely
make a fire. I had no cause
to feel the weight I felt
inside those walls
when rum refused me words
and no amount of it
and nothing, would shake them
from the thickets of my mind
and bend them to the page

Sex

the tyranny of flesh
in bodies new and young
caution not a thing yet
the speed of it, the danger
keys unlocking doors
in unmapped places
midnight in strange buildings
elevators opening
and closing, the taste
of lipstick, smoke and menthol
stairwells hot with breath
and exit lights
fumbled knobs and switches
gold bands giving way
clothing cast aside, thin scraps
of lovely colour on the floor
the texture of rough carpet
curtains never seen or drawn
a balcony somewhere
the grasp of heat and hands
a wine glass
tipped and breaking
shoes askew
flesh a torrent tumbling
that whole insatiable sky
of fireworks exploding
I travelled much
that way in Lowertown
and needed to, and needed to

Shadowland

Visitor

she came to see me once
before she flew to the coast
an afternoon knock at the door
I felt like a thief
with the goods in my hands
caught in the glare
of that spartan room
I'd chosen over her
but she had not come to intrude
just stood there
with all that I'd put in her eyes
and asked if I was sure
a ceremony of sorts
the unmaking of the riverbank
whole scrapbooks
floating away
in the pale thin brush of day
there was nothing I could say
that would help at all
a knife can't bind its wounds
I see the door, the way it closed
hear her footsteps walking away
she never did come back again
except in Dylan lines
which sailed like nails
through the light bulb air
and embedded in the plaster there

Quarts

the culture was quart bottles
on the Quebec side
no pissing around with pints
as in Ontario, beer washing
like the river in spring
through the low and lovely
places that we haunted
men and women
circling like stray boats
on swaying waters
bumping, crashing, laughing
in squalls of dirty dancing
as tempers
out of nowhere flashed
and were as quickly quelled
by pouncing bouncers
like the legend, Gerry Barber
who arranged
airfare for the foolish
to the parking lot
as waiters without ceasing
glided back and forth
and with a nod
set chilled Cinquante
and Molson Export
down before us
or extra strength Brador
no thought to dainty
craft brands in those days
just bottles tall and brown
like little Eiffel Towers
glinting through the room
cool to grasp and hold
and pour golden to a glass

Caretaker

apartment 28, with its
brown nameless door
was up a flight of stairs
and down a dim-lit hallway
where I often came and went
at odd hours of the day
encountering no one
but the caretaker, a moody man
who kept a smoky desk
in a corner basement room
and sometimes yelled
into the phone in a language
foreign to my ear
he collected rent each month
with dark-nailed hands
and a sliver of a smile that
bespoke what might replace it
should I be late or short
a woman who said nothing
often there beside him
in the corner of his corner
where he waved a flaming lighter
when he felt expansive
cigarette on purple lips
and now and then
acknowledged her
by pointing to her breasts
as if they were prize trophies
he'd gunned down in the hills

Cuisine

I cooked two meals
in the year that I was there
a slice or two of oily meat
from a can with a metal key
served on a plate
from a cupboard rarely opened
with frozen peas
and minute rice, boiled
on a stove with pallid rings
evoking occupants
who had been that way before
the first meal early on
the second some months later
when memory of the first
had dimmed
it was not a place for food
or anything unbottled
or unaccompanied by cigarettes
and the tiny flaring matches
that I brought back from the bars
I ate mainly at the diners
on Dalhousie
breakfast at all hours
with coffee, coffee, coffee
or hot sandwiches
with fries in sullen gravy
and lemon meringue pie
in mighty slices
billowing from a fork
like candy piled with snow

Bradley Street

after hours, when both sides
of the river had shut down
we sometimes went to Vanier
and drank at a blind pig there
up a hill on Bradley Street
where noiseless shadows fell
and moonlight wept
on dented cars
just off the *Avenue of Sin*
as Montreal Road was known as
in that wistful time
when *The Playmate* bloomed
with strippers, outwitting
prudish councillors
in their failing war on pleasure
and pizza splayed its neon call
dealers there in tinted cars
bikers rumbling in the night
that strip was never still
we knew a country place
a little farther on, where fiddles
sang in French and English
and the old Eastview Hotel
where on lucky nights
arrangements could be made
as last call blinked
but Bradley was the last stop
and we parked carefully there
knocking lightly at the door
and waiting
for a man named Brian
to squint through a tiny window
and in a single practiced motion
sweep us swiftly in
and click the lock behind

Men in Spring

grace can fall through air
and settle still as milkweed
in places unexpected
or kindness stir
from nowhere
through the cracks of earth
I'd go to a park nearby
in that nether time of year
when sunshine whispered spring
before winter was fully gone
and see men sprawled
in knitted hats on the brown
dead grass of April
sharing wine from a paper bag
a choir of tobacco voices
from the mission or Sally Ann
swearing at one another
or anyone who walked past
Spare change? Go to hell.
The pope can fuck himself.
Pass that over here.
helping one another up
and down, feeding scraps
of something to a dog
and when the afternoon
had tilted west
and day had waned
drifting off in ones and twos
to stations of the sidewalk
in search of evening change

Muhammad Ali

he was champion of the world
when the west was young
and satellites flew
through space-lit skies
in the flush of World War Two
Float like a butterfly
sting like a bee, his fists, his feet
a ballet that pulled everything
into the ring – race, politics, war
and so much more
Why are all the angels white?
Muslim means
one who surrenders to god
I am America ... get used to me
he banished the bear
that Liston was
to claim the heavyweight crown
and won in the courts
when they stripped it away
for scorning the U.S. Army
I ain't got no quarrel
with them Viet Cong
left Nixon on the canvas
with Quarry and Foreman
declared service to others
the rent you pay
for your room on earth
and gave birth to rap
with eyes so mischievous
they made wisdom clear
I done wrestled with an alligator
... tussled with a whale
handcuffed lightning
put *thunder in jail*
and on the night of nights
that he stopped Joe Frazier

in the *Thrilla from Manilla*
with a billion watching
all over the earth
I saw Al throw his hands
in the midnight air
and dance a crazed *Ali shuffle*
on the sidewalks of Hull

Glass

broken glass lay everywhere
in Lowertown, or seemed to
in the diamond breath of dawn
flashing up from sidewalks
shattered next to hydro poles
and storm grates
teeth knocked
from the mouth of night
and left for street machines
to sweep away, or merchants
with their brooms
heads down at morning
muttering futile oaths
not unlike the scrawl I'd find
in notebooks after listening
for hours to *Desolation Row*
that searing sound
of Dylan in those days
which was less song or lyric
than a place I went
to bend the crowbars of my mind
that realm of Ezra Pound
and T. S. Eliot
fighting in the captain's tower
of kerosene and heart attacks
and a benzedrine harmonica
that so took me hostage
I wanted never to return
but genius can't be borrowed
or mimicked worth a damn
those pages in the morning
were the ink of broken glass

Buses

how they bulled their way
along those crisscross streets
the hands of drivers flying
at the wheel, engines
roaring in all seasons
great liners, red and white
plying asphalt waters
air brakes hissing
full of menace
cutting in and out of traffic
the flap and clunk of doors
closing without warning
amber ever flashing
as trash washed back on sidewalks
in their wake, or slush
splashed up from wheels
but now and then
I'd see them after storms
when all was white
labouring up the hill
by the Chateau Laurier
impotent as eels
fishtailing to exhaustion
in the glorious grip of winter
and I'd lift my boots
like spoons from perfect frosting
and stride past
as if they were not there

The Age of Print

it was the time of newspapers
when words had weight and worth
the scent of ink on newsprint
and tobacco smoke
at newsstands
where proprietors in coats
rubbed hands for warmth in winter
doors ever opening
and closing in the cold
I'd step in there and feel
the world draw in
the *Citizen* and *Journal*
headlines bold and jarring
columns packed with news
photos black and white
leaping bright as colour
from the page
the *Globe and Mail* of Bay Street
and the brash *Toronto Star*
bristling with bright prose
papers east and papers west
the *Gazette* and the other *Star*
from the city of the saints
La Presse, Le Droit
Le Journal de Montréal
the *Chronicle-Herald* from Halifax
and the *Telegram* from St. John's
the *Province* of Vancouver
and all the tabloid *Suns*
awash with crime and pin-up girls
or when the weekend came
the heavy, hallowed
Sunday New York Times
which I carried back as food
and fed myself with beer
and burning cigarettes
inside that Friel Street room

Night Sound

the city came to visit late
on summer evenings
when my window was ajar
sirens, sirens, sirens
wailing along the straightaway
of Rideau Street
fire, police and ambulance
muscle cars, scorching
asphalt out of nowhere
motorcycles, blurting
through the back streets
and voices, always voices
straggling back from bars
laughter mixed with cursing
the Francophones swore best
tabarnak, câlice, sacrament
their effortless translation
of the sacred to the profane
we Anglos dull beside them
with our tiresome torrent
of *fuck this or that or you*
silence rare, though lulls
would sometimes settle
and I would hear the crunch
of pebbles under wheels
and motors shutting off
door locks turning in the dark
a dog somewhere
the chur of crickets
or the rhythms of the couple
from the window just below
before they slumped to sleep

Visions

I went unsettled places
in my dreams, tall buildings
with dark elevators that
would not descend to earth
the canal in winter
where I passed beneath
a bridge and fell through ice
to another country
a church where widows
in clothes of long ago
swept blackness out with brooms
and sang mysteriously
a corridor of light
where a figure without eyes
dissolved, and said
it would return
when I had solved the koan
animals looking down
on lives no longer theirs
and a car of wild laughter
with no one at the wheel
which stopped where I was
standing in the rain
and I would wake and blink
in a room with paper walls
and drink dark liquid
stirred with powder from a jar

Sisters

the Grey Nuns in their habit
I'd see them pass like
chimeras on the sidewalk
sisters of such charity
attending to the sick and poor
silver crosses swaying
in the wind, and I'd wonder
were they really women
inside those clouds of cloth
faces all but hidden
feet scarcely there at all
beneath long swaying robes
how could they live
so cut off from the world
 – or sin, even if they wanted to
could anyone
really last a lifetime
without yielding to temptation
and did they never ponder
in the great aloneness
of the mother house at night
what was happening
all about them in the dim-lit
dens of Lowertown
or lift their eyes unto the lights
across the river and consider
the carnival there
the bodies and the bars
and not wish
to cross that bridge just once
and stroll the wild main of Hull

Grace

mercy doesn't fall, it floats
where needed most
I never knew a church
when I was there, but I would
feel the presence
of *St. Brigid's* and *Notre Dame*
each time I walked that way
the way they reared into the sky
silence seeping down
the toll of bells
for weddings and for funerals
that sense of ceremony
and great occasion
the glide of limousines
for cardinals, for criminals
the mystery of faith
and the democracy of mass
for one and all
the manner of good Catholics
as they climbed
those steps at morning
in pain and grief and gratitude
retreating into silence
within those great stone walls
and the calm that filtered out
through high imposing doors
the lap of waves
that makes stone smooth

Moments

She

there was a woman
lovely as a storm
who came into that time
and broke shadows into light
and took me off
to that mysterious shore
which makes a woman sex
and sex a woman
with such exquisite fury
that even as it happens
she may not know
her alchemy
or be certain she could
cast that spell again
the ache of it, the heat
a blaze that burned
through nooks of summer
and made hot secrets
for a while, and fled
to woods and darkened paths
and brimmed with alcohol
and put a gleam inside my room
as he waited out
her absence
until the season broke
and she returned to him

The Hill

logs still floated on the river
as if the spell
of centennial year
had never come at all
brooding booms of timber
afloat below the falls
the putrid mill still there
on the opposite shore
its stench ever on the air
reaching in certain winds
even to the marble halls
of Parliament
a scene depicted
by the Bank of Canada
on its final dollar bill
tugboats wrestling logs
on roiled waters
before the note became a coin
and the mill shut down
I'd ride up there at night
on my motorcycle
which was still allowed then
before terrorism came
and park in the muted glow
of the Library of Parliament
and walk along the iron rail
and see swirls of great pollution
on currents dark below
and I'd wonder in the solitude
that ached along that bluff
what would become of Canada
and me

The Hour

the late night had a stillness
not entirely concealed
by the city and its noise
I'd feel it in the parking spots
along Dalhousie at four a.m.
or in cones of yellow streetlight
where insects danced
and in the tapping of my boots
as I walked to the diner door
and sat among lone figures
at the counter
as they opened little packets
of jam and peanut butter
and spread the contents out
to the edges of warm toast
or lifted steaming mugs
and placed them down again
more quietly than at other
times of day, the sound
of cutlery on plates
words like sparrows rising
in the flat fluorescent light
more coffee?
yes please, thank you
a liturgy, almost church-like
as if to hold a spell
or something, for a while

The Eating Houses

Doc Ballantyne died that fall
in his 94th year and was buried
with the builders of the capital
at Beechwood Cemetery
a bulky man, blond with a
ruddy face and out-sized nose
an immigrant from Glasgow
who loved the night
and opened *Boston Lunch*
on Sparks Street in 1909
the city's first all-night diner
beans and pie
like mother made
we never close
a nickel for a steaming plate
the same for thick cream pie
the haunt of cops
in clomping boots
of fire and railway men
and lost souls
lurching out of darkness
with alcohol on their breath
slumping into shelf chairs
to share a word with Doc
or genial Scottie Whyte who
served long behind the counter
the *eating house* that
showed the way for all the others
Uwanta Lunch on Bank Street
the *Metropole* and *Victory*
The Russell and *Grand Trunk*
Karson's, *Mack's* and *Dairy Lunch*
across the reach of time
to the old *New Moon* and *Mellos*
alight in quivering shadows
and the feel of all things lonesome
in the valley of the night

Melancholy

the thing with melancholy
is that it tiptoes in
and then ... is there
as if it had not been away
a mist, a thin gray rain
that found fault with my poetry
or reminded me of words
I might have said
in fumbled moments past
I'd feel it creep
down byways to my fingertips
and linger there
like shadows cast by oil lamps
in parlours long ago
or stalk me with a song
that coiled like thread
around a spool
I'd be the drunk
in Cohen's midnight choir
or skid in city shoes
on Tyson's summer towboats
or hear Lightfoot's jet plane roar
down *Runway No. 9*
and I'd feel
pinpricks on my skin
and lift my eyes and look away

Letters

we kept in touch
enough to not dishonour
what had passed
between us in our time
no calls, too keen a thing
but letters now and then
when letters flew like birds
to distant windowsills
and words had greater weight
than light motes on a screen
they were events of a sort
creations of pen on paper
sealed inside white envelopes
with postage in the upper
right hand corner
the portrait of the queen
in earrings and a crown
eight cents, first class
to anywhere
in the vast
the all but limitless
geography of Canada
for she had moved by then
to the interior
and was teaching kids again
the pang at that familiar writing
in the mailbox, the feel of it
her careful restrained lines
and the search
when I sat down
at the table in that room
for words to send back in reply
respectful of my place
in what I had put asunder

Nixon

the night Nixon resigned
or announced that he'd be gone
by noon the following day
I stood in a bar with Al
and we raised our glasses
to the man who peered out
punch drunk
from the screen, our hearts
soaring in a moment
that felt good and right
this president
who personified the bomb
the draft, the beehive hairdo
hold of the 1950s
of McCarthy and Jim Crow
and policemen clubbing back
resistance to his war
the endless war in Vietnam
the whole unholy mess
of everything we'd pitched
into the incinerator
of that dark and gnarled visage
gone as sunset sank
in the fool's gold dusk
of that indelible August night
idealism, if fervent enough
for long enough
it seemed
in that sweet moment
might prevail
sobriety was for the morning

Of the Mind

I knew a place where
Lawrence Ferlinghetti
came to visit with the Beats
from Greenwich Village
and brought books from
City Lights in San Francisco
Allen Ginsberg intoning *Howl*
Orlovsky at his side
and Kerouac, always Kerouac
with Joyce Johnson for a time
home from the hurting roads
of big America with its
forever aching bus stops
and endless blacktop miles
William Burroughs
Gregory Corso
beards, berets and bongo drums
Carolyn Cassady, with Neal
half crazed on speed again
and a little later on
the waif from the Iron Range
who sang of a girl
from the north country fair
and played at *Cafe Wha?* for
basket change
before *Hard Rain*
and *Like a Rolling Stone*
we go a million places
for warmth on dank chill nights
this was one of mine

Coins

they jingled in our blue jeans
then, pennies, nickels,
dimes and quarters
before plastic cards prevailed
or cell phones were imagined
the sound, the sight
the weight of them in pockets
when men stood up
or women emptied purses
coins tumbling out with lighters
combs and lipstick tubes
clattering onto counter tops
clinking into parking meters
or descending the cranky arteries
of vending machines
so many coins required
for candy bars or cigarettes
or chips in foil bags
the profanity in corridors
of lounges late at night
when items jammed
or change did not appear
palms clubbing metal casing
boots flashing out in anger
like the machine I kicked
one night in Hull
as Al and I were leaving
and coins came tumbling down
a glittering Niagara
to our astonished hands
so that we kicked again
and then again
until the contraption's dented udder
could produce no more
and we vanished in the night

Friends

we liked weed with lots of wine
in those unfurling days
Madawaska mindfuck
which Big Bill procured
from back-to-the-landers
in the Upper Ottawa Valley
and that on many a night
cured us, or LeDain
in clear smooth bags
which Jim and Ginette brought
back from New Brunswick
named by Jim himself
after the inquiry
into drug use at the time
and which they shared
to the blare
of *Acadian Driftwood*
the story of their ancestors
banished long ago
to bayous so far south
or the B.C. bud
that John and Ginny
transported over the Rockies
and hid in the ceiling
of the place they found
out Beechwood
on the edge of Vanier
hey, hey, we're on our way
how many brain cells
can we kill today
our bodies
young and indestructible
in that bright and little while

SAQ

on Saturday afternoons we
crossed the river in daylight
which felt odd
van tires humming
on the Interprovincial Bridge
John with a joint
already lit up, window ajar
to let fumes drift out
and we'd stock up on wine
at the *SAQ,* the largest
liquor store in West Quebec
gallon jugs
of red and white
with wire handles
that cut into our hands
and extra proof Brador
malt liquor, premium brewed
in cases blue and gold
and now and then
a litre of Alcool
which at 94%
was rocket fuel that
could flatten a rutting moose
we'd go all night, and most
of Sunday, and still somehow
show up for work on Monday

Passing

it passed so quickly
that season when our eyes
could fall on slender things
and make them shine
a candle on a bottle
flicking midnight at a wall
a Janis poster
brimming with the blues
or the *Sweetland Ave.* street sign
someone snatched at closing
one night in Sandy Hill
we'd walk with open coats
and matches in our hands
along the paths
of the park at Major's Hill
smoke trailing
on the autumn air
and scarcely see the naked trees
or hear the lament
of fallen leaves, boats gone
from the drained canal
the limestone eyes
of Parliament Hill upon us
the river already
stiffening for winter
seasons pass without appeal
and bonds that seem eternal
can snap like twigs
beneath the tramp of boots

Assenting

truth waits until the mind
grows still
and weariness sets in –
flecks of gold that make
a peace of sorts with time
I did not ponder much for long
in the whirl of those
swift days
for all was gilt in its own way
Lowertown
the tutor of bright bottle caps
in wrinkled tinfoil nights
or sex that blinked
and then
was gone
and placed a lovely ache
upon the seasons
and said how much
a room can hold

Farewell

Telephone

I moved to Centretown
not far from Al
and the charcoal fire escape
that always caught my eye
I climbed it once myself
when I had not been drinking
a rickety labyrinth upward
to a narrow door
that opened
into his book-strewn room
he laughed, and when I left
walked down the stairs with me
and stood where daylight
flared along the sidewalk
in slats of afternoon
and taxicabs coughed past
gesturing with an arm
and an ivory cigarette
and said with eyes that crackle yet
I give you poetry
and I turned to my new place
which had furniture I owned
a fridge with food
and a tree that I
could almost reach and touch
from my small balcony
and there one Sunday morning
when I was writing
the telephone rang, and a voice
I did not know I was
waiting for
said, *this is Susan*

And After That …

it's said that a man
is never the same
when a woman
has slept in his eyes
and painted her scent
on the skies of his flesh
and swept
lesser wisdoms away

The Bridge

when I go, I'll turn and look
a final time, that I might
take you with me
a billion coins of light
flashing in the current
below the iron bridge

where we stopped and
stood so often, and the sun
would find you there
reach past clouds
above the moody dam
and pour itself upon you

there among old girders
of rust and faded paint
where we mellowed
without resistance
in the soft, slow melt of time

and words walked lightly
on our tongues
or scarcely walked at all
as seasons settled
without marking
in the crevices of our days

and I'll hold that
like an old Matryoshka doll
and all the rest will be inside

Footnotes

Flight

Trumpets and Blue: I grew up in rural Nova Scotia and was married there to a young woman just out of teachers' college.

Ring Dance: We lived initially in Saint John, New Brunswick, before moving to Toronto and settling in Ottawa.

Gone: References *Angels and Devils the Following Day from Mythical Kings and Iguanas* by Dory Previn, 1971. (Mediaarts/United Artists).

Morrow: We lived on Cambridge Street South near the Queensway, which cuts through the heart Ottawa.

Night

Ink: The New Moon Restaurant at 271 Dalhousie Street no longer exists. An updated Mellos still operates at 290 Dalhousie Street.

Alan: A friend through life, Alan Strickland (b. September 20, 1943 – d. September 6, 2014).

Slow Dance: Paul Chartier died May 18, 1966, when a dynamite bomb he intended to throw onto the floor of the House of Commons exploded in a Parliament Hill washroom. He misjudged how long the fuse would burn.

Want Ads: Personal ads, various dates, *The Ottawa Citizen*, and *The Ottawa Journal*, 1974.

Trial: Provincial Court, Province of Quebec, District of Hull, No. 550-01-1732-75, Regina vs. David Ward Blaikie, February 6th, 1976: "On or about June 13th, 1975 . . . did illegally and volontary (sic) obstruct a police officer in the performance of his duties by resisting to his own arrest . . ."

Spirits

Jack: Quotation adapted from *On The Road* by Jack Kerouac, Viking Press, 1957.

Tangled: References various recordings from *Blood on the Tracks*, Bob Dylan, Columbia Records, 1975.

Saigon: References Walter Cronkite, anchor of the CBS Evening News (1962-1981), and Johnny Cash, *The Man in Black*, Columbia Records, 1971.

Friel Street: References The Ottawa Citizen – October 22, 1974, p.3; October 28, 1974, p.1; December 16, 1974, p.5; February 26, 1976, p.2; October 31, 1974, p.3; November 25, 1975, p.18.

Passage: References *This Storm Shall Surely Pass* from *With Pleasure*, Fraser & DeBolt, Columbia Records, 1973.

Apparitions: The 200-kilometre Rideau Canal, connecting Ottawa with the St. Lawrence River at Kingston, was completed between 1826 and 1832 as an alternate shipping route in the event of war between Canada and the U.S.

Shadowland

Quarts: Gerald Emmett (Gerry) Barber (b. August 14, 1929 – d. May 27, 1984) was a bouncer at bars and nightclubs for thirty years in West Quebec, surviving gun, knife, tire iron and baseball bat attacks. He died of heart failure – dancing.

Men in Spring: Homeless shelters have long been part of Lowertown, including the Ottawa Mission, the Shepherds of Good Hope and the Men's Hostel, run by the Salvation Army.

Muhammad Ali: Quotations from Sky Sports, June 5, 2016; O, The Oprah Magazine, June 2001; Bleacher Report, Jonathan Duffy, June 28, 2009.

Glass: Eleven minutes long, *Desolation Row* first appeared on *Highway 61 Revisited*, Bob Dylan, 1965, Columbia Records.

Grace: Notre Dame Cathedral dates back to 1839, decades before Canada became a country. St. Brigid's was built in 1892, primarily as a place of worship for Irish Catholics. It closed in 2006 but survives today as Saint Brigid's Centre for the Arts.

Sisters: The Congregation of the Sisters of Charity of Ottawa (better known as Grey Nuns of the Cross) celebrated 175 years in Ottawa in 2020. Within their first three months in Bytown (as the city was first known) they opened a bilingual school, a general hospital, an orphanage, and a home for the elderly.

The Eating Houses: George (Doc) Ballantyne, *The Ottawa Journal,* September 21, 1974, p.32; *Below the Hill,* Dave Brown, The Ottawa Journal, October 3, 1974, p.20; Over My Shoulder, The Evening Citizen, January 31, 1953, Section 3, p.2.

Moments

Melancholy: References *Bird on the Wire* (Leonard Cohen, Columbia Records, 1969), *Summer Wages* (Ian Tyson and Sylvia Tyson, Vanguard Records, 1969) and *Early Morning Rain* (Gordon Lightfoot, United Artists, 1966).

Nixon: On the evening of August 8, 1974, Richard Nixon announced he would resign as President of the United States at noon on the following day.

Of the Mind: Lawrence Ferlinghetti published *A Coney Island of the Mind* in 1958 (New Directions Publishing). More than one million copies have been printed. It has been translated into a dozen languages.

Friends: References *Acadian Driftwood*, The Band (Shangri-la Studio), 1975.

Passing: References Janis Joplin (b. January 19, 1943 – d. October 4, 1970).

Farewell

The Bridge: With love and gratitude to Susan Rosidi.

David Blaikie on Writing

Writing baffles me, though I've been at it all my life, and have kept a daily diary for more than forty years. It's a bit like baking bread. I knead the keys and words rise up, most of them unremarkable – letters, email, journals, decades of newspaper articles, the everyday prose of the communications field. Yet there is a value to all writing, if only a reminder to the fingertips, that anything worth saying is worth saying well. The challenge is ever there.

Poetry is another matter – elusive, mysterious, arriving from who knows where. The older I get the more I'm convinced that poetry is a gift and poets are the channels through which it flows. It cannot be coerced, without diluting it, yet demands all the craft that we can muster to bring it to the page. My influences over the years have been many. A few stand out – Alden Nowlan and Patrick Lane, Jack Kerouac and Henry David Thoreau, plus a host of great musician/writers of my time, Bob Dylan, Leonard Cohen, Joni Mitchell, Patti Smith.

All my life I've looked for tricks to make it easier – alcohol, music, meditation. Nothing very reliable has emerged, except one thing. Walking seems to help. A powerful link exists between mind and body and walking seems to clarify the path between the two, at least for me. That's all I know. I was a marathon runner in my younger years. I still try to walk an hour a day.

David Blaikie Bio Notes

David Blaikie is a journalist and writer who grew up in Nova Scotia and reported for the *Truro Daily News, The Canadian Press, The Toronto Star* and *Reuters*. He spent eighteen years in the Parliamentary Press Gallery and had a second career in labour communications. He has published three volumes of poetry, *Her Final Days*, the story of his mother who died of AIDS after a blood transfusion in the 1980s; *Farewell to Coney Island*, winner of the inaugural chapbook award of the Tree Reading Series in Ottawa (2011) and *In that Old City by the Sea* (2017). He lives in Ottawa.

www.ingramcontent.com/pod-product-compliance
Lightning Source LLC
Chambersburg PA
CBHW031244120626
46545CB00007B/2645